SALAD JAIL

This cookbook of gluten-free recipes will get you out of salad jail. Don't get me wrong - salad rocks! It just gets old when it seems like the only thing available on restaurant menus and in cookbooks for people with a gluten issue is the rabbit food.

These are foods that my kids will eat – and brag about to their friends

I look like a gourmet without the stomach distress

Some of it is even healthy

Read the entire recipe before buying anything or starting any of the steps.

I don't always measure out the ingredients – be brave!

You'll figure it out!

D1406831

Brisket Chili

Buy a fresh brisket (half or whole) from a meat market. Don't get a frozen one. Don't freeze it. Buy it and smoke it within a couple of days of purchase, following the Brisket Rub recipe in this cookbook.

If you don't have a whole day to spend managing the smoker, you can cut it into a few large pieces, season it with steak seasoning, and cram it into your crock pot with some water. Cook it on low for the day.

Smoked is better, if you have the time, but the crockpot version works well too for this chili recipe.

Smoke it until it's done using whatever smoker apparatus you've got and whatever instructions go with it. Plan for it to take all day. Brisket should be smoked slowly over time. If you hurry it, it will dry out.

Eat some! Great with Barbecue Sauce (see recipe)!

Put the remaining brisket, fat and all, into a crock pot.

Add some water so it doesn't dry out.

Add into crock pot:

1 diced yellow or white onion (NOT a red onion and NOT a Vidalia onion)
3 or 4 minced garlic cloves
1 handful of chopped fresh parsley
1 handful of chopped fresh oregano
3 or 4 whole fresh or frozen chili peppers
1-2 cans of beans (your choice – we like kidney beans for this recipe)
1 can of tomato sauce (regular kind without any extra seasonings in it)
DO NOT SUB TOMATO PASTE ~ack~
1 chocolate bar (we used a Hershey bar, but any milk chocolate will do)
Liberal sprinkle of cinnamon
Liberal sprinkle of black pepper
Liberal sprinkle of chipotle powder
Liberal sprinkle of Kosher salt

Leave crock pot on low all day and enjoy!

Can add more salt & chipotle powder when serving

We include shredded cheese, sour cream, and diced green onions when we serve this dish.

We don't include noodles, because that's just wrong.

Warms up great for leftovers and you can freeze it and thaw it out later if you made more than you can eat in a week.

Wins camping chili contests!

Brisket Rub

Thyme leaves (a lot)
Sage leaves (a lot)
Oregano leaves (less)
Rosemary (less)
Kosher salt (less)
Brown sugar (a lot)
Ground black pepper (less)
Grated lemon peel (less)

Fresh is better, but dried herbs also work in this recipe.

OK, so I don't always have measurements. You won't need them. The combination of flavors is what matters; moreover, the volume of each ingredient that you need actually depends on the size of the brisket.

Buy the brisket fresh and cook it fresh. Don't buy it frozen and don't freeze it. This is important, which is why it's in here twice.

The rub should cover entire brisket. Smoke it until it is done.

Leftover brisket can be used to make Brisket Chili.

Barbecue Sauce

Apple cider vinegar
Dark brown sugar
Sorghum
Molasses
Coriander
Chili pepper flakes
smoked paprika
smoked salt
smoked black pepper
Apple juice
Ground allspice
Ground cloves
Sesame seed oil
Arrowroot (thickener)

I don't really have specific volumes. If you are making a gallon, use more of the spices (except for the apple cider vinegar - a little bit goes a long way).

My rule of thumb for apple cider vinegar is this: use equal amounts of a sweetener with it (like honey, like dark brown sugar, like sorghum, like molasses). It is very, very tart. Healthy for you according to the package, but TART.

Combine all but the arrowroot in a sauce pan. Bring to a boil. Reduce by half on medium/high heat. Reduce to simmer. Scoop out a half cup of the sauce. Add arrowroot to the half cup. NEVER sprinkle the dry arrowroot directly to the contents of the sauce pan. Combine. Return to sauce pan. Simmer until saucy. Keeps nicely.

Rib Rub

<Coriander
<Allspice
>Black pepper
<Garlic granules
>Cumin
>Brown sugar
<Thyme
<Rosemary
<Grated lemon peel
<Seasoned salt

< is less
> Is more

The volume of each ingredient you use depends on the amount of ribs you intend to grill.

I like fresh herbs but the dried kind will do here too.

Add all together and rub on pork ribs. Grill or smoke until done and the rub looks like bark.

Chicken Saltimbocca

Several boneless, skinless chicken breasts
Slices of mozzarella or provolone (one per chicken breast)
Slices of pancetta or speck (one per chicken breast)
DO NOT SUB PROSCUITTO
Regular size jar of marinara sauce
About a cup of large, whole, fresh sage leaves
Olive oil
Salt & pepper
Parmesan cheese

The picture shows the specific items used but any brand will do for this recipe. The wine is for afterwards if you are over 21; do not add it into your dish!

Coat a glass baking dish with olive oil.

Dip chicken breasts in the olive oil that is in the dish, coating both sides.

Salt and pepper the chicken breasts.

Lay each chicken breast on a slice of pancetta or speck, then top with fresh sage leaves.

Add a slice of mozzarella or provolone on top of each chicken breast.

Pour the marinara sauce over all, then sprinkle the chicken breasts with parmesan cheese.

It's kinda like Chicken Parmesan, but the sage leaves give it an awesome unique flavor and the pancetta adds some saltiness.

Bake for around 30 minutes at 375 degrees F or until chicken is completely cooked per a meat thermometer.

Enjoy with a good dry red wine (if you are over 21!)

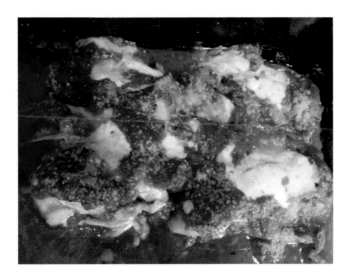

Roast Beast

This yummy recipe is good for any time of the year; don't save it until the night before Christmas!

Rib roast or full rack of lamb or some other red meat with bones (expensive stuff, don't go cheap on the meat)

Minced garlic
Minced oregano
smoked pepper
Kosher salt
Turmeric (go easy on it)
Water

Make a rub with just enough water for it all to stick together

Put all over meat

READ how to use the salt block on your grill and follow those instructions. You'll need a safe method to get the hot salt block with your finished meat off the grill. Plan ahead and time it so you can turn off the grill and let it cool somewhat. We have long tongs and a fire resistant oven mitt that goes halfway up your arm. And we turn off the grill first. We don't try removing that salt block while the grill is still super hot.

Roast meat on a salt block on the grill according to directions on the salt block package.

You can cut and serve it on the salt block as well but know that it will continue to cook your meat as it sits on it.

Ribeye Roast on Salt Block

"Roast Beast 2.0"

Sage leaves
Rosemary leaves
Minced garlic (8 cloves)
smoked salt
Pepper
Ground coriander
Nutmeg
Ground black truffle

Slather butter on all sides of ribeye roast before smashing the rub in.

USE REAL BUTTER.

Roast on salt block on the grill. See Roast Beast recipe for specific instructions on the salt block grilling process.

Pork Chop Glaze

Honey
Sorghum
Ground allspice
Ground nutmeg
Gran Marnier or other orange liqueur
Gluten-free soy sauce
Chipotle powder
Coarse salt
Smoked pepper
Apple cider vinegar (anywhere you see this item, use sparingly)

Orange liqueur is an awesome cooking ingredient that you'll see in multiple recipes, but don't drink it warm, from the bottle, during a Colts football game. Ack.

Put all on pork, roast in oven or on grill.

Serve with some green foodstuffs like what you see in the picture. We like to roast the veggies alongside the pork chops.

Orange Chicken Sauce

2 tablespoons apple cider vinegar
½ cup brown sugar
5 shakes cumin
3 tablespoons fish sauce
2 tablespoons gluten free soy sauce
5 shakes nutmeg
Grated orange peel from 1 orange (dried kind is OK too)
1 teaspoon mint leaves, minced
2 squirts sriracha
1 tablespoon grated fresh gingerroot
Juice from 1 orange
1 tablespoon ground coriander

Sprinkle stir fry veggies with garlic granules while frying

Use canola oil sparingly to stir fry veggies and chicken

Add your orange chicken sauce to the pan

Serve

This is a good sauce made with ingredients that I usually have on hand.

Stir Fry Sauce

Good with chicken or pork

Brown sugar
Gluten free soy sauce
Mirin
Fish sauce
Sweet chili sauce
Lime juice
Cilantro

Lazy, but yummy

We like both Bragg's and Tamari, but any gluten free soy sauce will work in this recipe.

If you like making spring rolls or egg rolls, this recipe can also serve as the dipping sauce.

Cellophane Noodle Sauce

Mirin
Lime juice
Sriracha
Fish sauce
Gluten free soy sauce
Cornstarch
Ginger-garlic paste (there are thousands of recipes online for this – make a bunch and freeze it in an ice cube tray so it's available for use in this and other recipes)
Cilantro

Combine all and dip your finger in to taste. Adjust flavors as needed (sweet, bitter, salty, sour, and savory are all represented).

Follow package instructions for noodles, which are gluten-free.

Healing Tea

Tamarind paste
Cardamom
Dandelion root tea bag
Apple cider vinegar
Elderberry syrup
Dark brown sugar
Honey
Minced fresh gingerroot
Hot water

Kids don't believe it'll heal what ails them but who really knows? It is tasty and fragrant.

Best Guacamole

Many people over the years have agreed with me that this one is the best guac they've ever had. We love it so much that none of us will order guacamole from restaurants for fear of being disappointed.

3 ripe avocadoes
Juice of 1 lime
Kosher salt (go easy on it at first – you can add more later if it isn't salty enough)
Fresh ground black pepper (about a ½ teaspoon)
1 minced jalapeno pepper
1 minced cayenne or serrano pepper
1 diced yellow or white onion (DO NOT USE RED ONION OR VIDALIA ONION)
At least 3 tablespoons of chopped fresh cilantro leaves

Go heavy on the cilantro – more is better

Put all in a big plastic freezer bag and squish to combine. This bag method is my all-time favorite for dip-making. Kids will enjoy this job. When it is combined/squished properly, cut off a corner and squeeze it all into a container for storage. Keep the pits in it.

Store it with the pits evenly distributed in the guacamole – they will keep it green longer.

Serve with tortilla chips (our fave kind is pictured but any type of gluten free tortilla chip will work for this recipe), tacos, potato chips, etc. YUM

Cheese Ball

Brick of cream cheese
Bacon bits (about 7 slices)
1 tablespoon white vinegar
1 teaspoon onion powder
Chopped fresh or dried chives
Smoked salt

Mix cream cheese with bacon, vinegar, onion powder, then roll in chives and salt.

Roll it up into a ball using plastic wrap and refrigerate.

Serve with sturdy potato chips or salty gluten-free crackers.

Don't go light on the salt - you will need it to counter the white vinegar.

Bacon Wrapped Dates

Medjool dates, pitted
Havarti cheese
Dry andouille sausage links
Bacon
Smoked pepper

Sauce: equal parts sriracha, smoky barbecue sauce, and Gran Marnier or other orange liqueur

Cut open and stuff the dates with cheese and andouille slices, then wrap in bacon.

Arrange in glass pan.

Mix sauce and pour over dates.

Sprinkle with smoked pepper.

Bake 30-45 min on 350 degrees F.

Serve immediately.

Very rich, but the sauce helps to cut the sweetness of the dates.

Good for parties where everybody grabs one or two, and then POOF they are all gone before any of us can make ourself sick eating 15-20 of them.

Bacon Wrapped Scallops

Scallops (big ones)
Bacon (thin sliced)
Paprika
Maple syrup

Scallop sauce: equal parts sriracha, smoky barbecue sauce, Gran Marnier or other orange liqueur (I love this sauce!)

Coat scallops with maple syrup, wrap in bacon, then sprinkle with paprika.

Bake in glass pan in oven, fry in frying pan on stove, or grill until scallops are no longer translucent and bacon is reasonably cooked.

Tailgate Scallops

2 tablespoons grape seed oil
½ cup plum wine
1 tablespoon paprika
1 tablespoon adobo seasoning (you can use a seafood seasoning like Old Bay if the MSG doesn't bother you)
2 tablespoons gluten free soy sauce
1 tablespoon brown sugar
1 tablespoon lemon juice
1 pound bay scallops

Combine ingredients
Marinate scallops overnight
Heat griddle over grill
Fry on very high heat until translucent, turning once

It won't take very long at all – PAY ATTENTION to the scallops and remove them as soon as they are no longer translucent. If you over cook them they will get rubbery.

Serve immediately.

Alfredo Sauce

Heavy cream
Butter (the real stuff, NOT margarine)
Grated parmesan cheese
White pepper
Garlic salt
Dash of nutmeg
Some other type of hard white cheese, grated or shredded (mild white cheddar or similar)

Don't use a soft cheese like cream cheese, goat cheese or mozzarella.

Melt butter over medium heat.
When it is melted, add heavy cream, garlic salt, and white pepper. Stir often.
When it is warm, gradually add cheese, stirring until melted and creamy.

Reduce heat to low. Add nutmeg. Serve with gluten free pasta (I like the kind made with corn over the kind made with rice because it cooks and tastes similar to the real thing).

It keeps, but because it is all dairy, it will harden. It will be completely hard in the refrigerator and you'll need to warm it up in a sauce pan or in the microwave to make it look "saucy" again.

I usually don't end up with leftovers. If we run out of pasta before we run out of this sauce, the kids and my husband will toast bread and eat the rest of it on toasted bread.

Hollandaise Sauce

3 egg yolks
1 tablespoon lemon juice
½ cup softened butter (NOT MARGARINE)

In a sauce pan, stir egg yolks and lemon juice with a wire whisk

Add ¼ cup of the softened butter

Heat over VERY LOW heat, stirring constantly with the whisk, until butter is melted.

Add remaining ¼ cup of the softened butter. Continue stirring until the butter is melted and the sauce has thickened. SLOW is key. If you heat it too fast, you'll cook your eggs and the sauce will look curdy. Still tastes OK but looks like shit.

Serve immediately. It won't keep. Eat it all.

Macadamia-Crusted Sea Bass or Mahi Mahi with Butter Wine Sauce

For the wine sauce:
1 stick of butter (NOT margarine)
½ tsp garlic salt
1/8 tsp white pepper
¾ cup dry white wine (like a sauvignon blanc or pinot griglio)
DO NOT USE CHARDONNAY
½ cup heavy cream
1 tsp lemon juice
Up to 1 cup grated and/or shredded parmesan cheese

Melt butter in sauce pan over medium heat. Add garlic salt and white pepper. Stir to blend. Add heavy cream and simmer 15 minutes, adding parmesan cheese until creamy consistency is reached. Add wine and lemon juice. Remove from heat and set aside.

For the sea bass or mahi mahi:

4-8 oz sea bass fillets (no skin) or mahi mahi
If you have to buy them with skin, cut all of the skin off and feel with your fingers each fillet inch by inch to ensure no bones. Cut any bones out.

¾ cup grated parmesan cheese
8 oz macadamia nuts, coarsely chopped
4 tablespoons melted butter (NOT MARGARINE)
4 tsp olive oil
Salt and pepper
1-2 cups brown rice, prepared according to package instructions
Lemon wedges

Preheat oven to 350 degrees F. Butter a rectangular glass baking dish.

Arrange fish fillets in pan and sprinkle liberally with salt and pepper.

Run macadamias through a chopper to coarsely grind/chop, then combine with parmesan cheese and melted butter.

Gently press macadamia-parmesan mixture onto fillets.

Drizzle 1 tsp olive oil on each fillet.

Bake the fillets until cooked through, about 20-25 minutes, depending on the thickness of the fish. Cut one of the thicker fillets open to see if it is flaky on the inside before serving to ensure they are all done.

Preheat broiler to high. Broil fish fillets on high until crust is golden brown, about 2 minutes.

Serve atop brown rice with prepared butter wine sauce and lemon wedges.

Goes nicely with the same dry white wine you used for the sauce if you are over 21.

Cheese Fondue

2 cups chicken broth
2 bay leaves
2 garlic cloves, minced
½ tsp whole white peppercorns
1 dried truffle
½ tsp truffle oil
Dash of nutmeg
4-6 oz wedge gruyere cheese
4-6 oz wedge fontina cheese
½ cup grated parmesan
1 cup mozzarella
¼ cup gluten free flour

Grate the cheeses
Boil the chicken broth with bay leaves, garlic, peppercorns, dried truffle, truffle oil and nutmeg 10-15 minutes

Remove the bay leaves.

Combine cheeses with flour and drop by handful into broth to melt.

Serve with veggies, fruits, breads, some nice wine if you are over 21.

I have a fondue pot and those fancy little forks but it's a pain in the ass to clean so I usually just leave the fondue in the sauce pan and set it on a hot pad. Not too classy but the clean up is easier and it tastes just as good.

Better yet, if it cools and hardens before you are done eating it, you can just put the sauce pan back on the stove top to warm it up!

Mayo Halibut

This sounds gross, but my kids really LOVE it

Halibut fillets
Mayonnaise (at least 1/4 cup per fillet)
Several minced garlic cloves (at least 1 per fillet)
Olive oil (about a tbsp per fillet)
Sea salt (about 1/8 tsp per fillet)
Pepper

Coat a glass baking pan with olive oil
Lay fillets in pan, coating with olive oil on all sides
Whisk salt with garlic cloves and olive oil
Salt and pepper the fillets liberally
Mix olive oil mixture with mayonnaise

Use real mayonnaise, not Miracle Whip, for this recipe.

Smear mayo-olive oil mixture on all sides and on top of fillets.

Bake at 350 degrees F for 20-30 minutes until fish is cooked through and mayo-olive oil mixture is golden brown. Cut into one of the thicker fillets to see if the insides are flaky before serving.

They fight over who gets to "pick first" from the baking pan when this dish is done cooking.

Bacon Wrapped Filet Bites

We change this one a lot
Not all of the ingredients really matter … some are just tradition …
Fresh sage is important
Worcestershire sauce is important, even if you can't say it right
Truffle salt is important
Garlic cloves are important
Rubbed sage (lots of it) is important

4 beef filets, cut into thirds
12 slices of bacon (thin or regular sliced)

Wrap the filet bites in bacon.
Each third of a filet gets a whole slice of bacon.

Put in the fridge to chill.

Mince 6-7 cloves of garlic
Chop at least ½ cup of fresh sage leaves
1 teaspoon truffle salt
½ cup Worcestershire sauce
1-2 tablespoons rubbed sage or more (go heavy on this ingredient)
Liberal sprinkle of nutmeg
½ teaspoon garlic salt (or more)
2 tablespoons olive oil
½ teaspoon lemon juice
Salt and pepper

DO NOT REFRIGERATE THE MARINADE

Before grilling, let bacon wrapped filet bites sit out and warm up (about 30 min)

Warm up the grill and get it ready for cooking

Pour marinade on filet bites and let sit 10 minutes
DO NOT LET IT SIT LONGER as it will overwhelm the filet bites

Grill to desired done-ness – we recommend medium rare

Eat ASAP!

If you don't want the burnt portions that you see in the photo below, leave out the olive oil.

Best Garlic Hummus

My kids like this way better than store-bought hummus.

This hummus is yummus.

We like garlic A LOT, so the recipe includes more garlic than maybe you all might want to use

Up to you

Garlic ROCKS

2 cans garbanzo beans (aka chickpeas)
SAVE the liquid from the can; do not discard it
½ cup extra virgin olive oil
6-8 cloves of garlic (or a whole head of it!)
1 tablespoon ground cumin
Juice of 1 lemon
Sea salt and black pepper
Chopped fresh parsley leaves

The picture shows the items we used but any brands will work for this recipe.

Roll the lemon on a counter top to soften it before cutting. Squeeze the juice into a food processor, turning the lemon slices inside out to get all of the juice from them. Remove any seeds before proceeding to the next step.

Add in all other ingredients except the parsley. SAVE the juice from the bean cans but don't put it in yet. You may need it later if the consistency of your hummus needs to be adjusted.

Add sea salt and black pepper to taste. I like salt a lot, but recommend going easy on it until you've tasted it. You can always add more salt later if you didn't add enough initially.

Process to a paste/sauce. Adjust consistency if needed by adding in a little of the bean juice.

Sprinkle parsley on top and a little more ground cumin.

Serve with gluten free crackers, potato chips, veggies, gluten free pretzels, etc.

Keeps well in the fridge.

Best Pork and Beans

I had always thought of pork & beans as "poor people food" when I was a kid. I came from a poor family, and pork & beans was a dish served often at my house. I hated beans. The texture was icky, the taste was bland, and I didn't care that it was good for me. I didn't care that it was a protein-y way to stretch the meat further so it fed more people.

This version ROCKS

Ingredients:

½ cup fresh parsley
Slab of unsliced jowl bacon
Mixed small potatoes (around 10)
1 can great northern beans
½ stick of butter (NOT MARGARINE)
4 oz goat cheese
Smoked pepper
½ cup water

Cook the jowl bacon in a crock pot on low all day with ½ cup of water. Save the broth.

Melt 1 tablespoon of butter in with the broth. Pour broth over the beans and warm up the beans in a sauce pan.

Cook potatoes in a bowl in the microwave 10 minutes, serve over parsley, butter pat, 1 tablespoon of goat cheese per plate. Add some beans to plate. Slice jowl bacon, add slice to plate and pour broth over all. Add pepper.

Tom's Ham

This is a family tradition. Odd that we'd be cooking a fully cooked ham
for 12 hours, but it's totally worth it! Best ham ever!

Get a fully cooked butt half ham. Not the shoulder or the picnic, but the butt portion. And it has to be fully cooked.

Handful or two of whole cloves
Pineapple slices in heavy syrup (15 oz can)
Brown sugar (as much as will dissolve in the juice that comes from the pineapple can)

Score the ham cross-ways with a knife and stick the cloves in the Xs that you make.

Put the ham flat side down in a clay pot.

If you don't have a clay pot, get one. Absolute necessity.
Lay pineapple rings on the ham.

Mix pineapple juice with brown sugar and pour over ham.
Bake 10-12 hours on 215 degrees F.

When it is done, you can just pull the bone right out, and the house will smell like heaven.

Duck Booby

You have to say it like "Ricky Booby" from that silly movie with Will Ferrell about NASCAR.

I tried making up other names over the years for this tasty, elegant dish,
but every time I make it, my kids call it "Duck Booby."

So, it's stuck. Sad. But tastes REALLY good.

Brands pictured are what we used but any brands will work for this recipe.

Ingredients:

Fennel seed, crushed in pestle
Rosemary (fresh is best)
Minced garlic
Sage leaves, chopped
Pairs of duck breasts
Shiitake or cremini mushrooms, sliced, stems removed
Extra virgin olive oil

Salt
Pepper

Sprinkle duck breasts liberally with salt & pepper

Combine fennel, rosemary, garlic, sage leaves, and olive oil to make a paste.

Preheat oven to 400 degrees F.

Place sliced mushrooms and herb paste over 1 duck breast. Put 2nd duck breast on top (meaty sides together) and tie with cooking string. Use a lot of string. Make sure they stay tied together, with most of the herb paste and mushrooms in between the duck breasts.

Heat a cast iron skillet on the stove top over medium-high heat. It will be HOT.

Brown the paired duck breasts (still tied together) on all sides, turning often, about 10 minutes.

If there is a lot of fat or oil in the cast iron skillet, take most of it out before putting the skillet with the duck breasts into the oven. MESS happens if you leave too much fat/oil in the skillet.

Bake about 25 minutes at 400 degrees F, turning the tied duck breasts occasionally.

Remove from oven, put on a plate with a lip or a pasta dish. Let rest 10 minutes. Cut cooking string off and discard. Cut duck into slices. Pour drippings from skillet over duck before serving.

Best Mashed Potatoes

Can there be such a thing? After all this time? My kids think so!

5 lb bag of Yukon Gold potatoes, peeled and chopped into small squares
Butter (the real thing, not margarine)
Goat Cheese or fromage
Salt

MOST IMPORTANT STEP: Salt the hell out of the water before you boil the potatoes in it. Seriously, dump in more salt than you think you need – at least 2 tablespoons! If you don't get enough salt now, you can't fix it later. Salt that water!!

Boil the potatoes in salt water for 10 minutes or until soft.

Put at least ½ stick of butter in the bottom of the mixing bowl with about the same amount of goat cheese or fromage.

I use a slotted wooden spoon to remove the boiled potatoes from the sauce pan into the mixing bowl, letting some of the water come over as well. Save the rest of the water for now in case your potatoes need a little more to be the right consistency.

The hot potatoes do a nice job of melting the butter and the goat cheese.

Run the mixer on low, then medium, then high. If the mashed potatoes don't look moist enough, add in a little more of the water.

When lumps are gone, transfer to an oven-safe bowl and add another ½ stick of butter (cut into slices) on top.

Warm in oven at 300 degrees F for a few minutes while you make the gravy. Or not. These mashed potatoes are so good they don't even NEED gravy.

Cornstarch Beef Stock Gravy

This is gross, but it tastes good. And it keeps in the fridge a few days, because it's not made from animal fat.

Beef stock (read the can instructions)
Cornstarch
Water
Salt

I don't like those cubes; I like the beef stock that is sort of a jelly-looking brown substance.

Dissolve beef stock into water per the instructions on the can. Go a little heavy on the beef stock for flavor. Add some salt.

Mix a tablespoon of cornstarch in ½ cup to 1 cup of COLD water until it dissolves.

Pour the cornstarch water into the beef stock. Stir continuously over medium heat until it looks like gravy, adjusting the temperature or amount of cornstarch water as needed until you get that gravy consistency. If you have to add cornstarch, do it by mixing it with COLD water. NEVER sprinkle dry cornstarch powder directly into your gravy.

Serve over potatoes, bread, roast, other stuff.

It sounds like a really cheap, crappy way to make gravy, but it tastes awesome and my kids love it. In fact, if I make real gravy from roast drippings, they are pissed off that it doesn't taste like this cornstarch beef stock gravy.

Chorizo

2 pounds ground pork (NOT the breakfast kind)
4 tablespoons chili powder (ground dried chili pepper)
2 tablespoons ground paprika
2 tablespoons dried oregano or 1 tablespoon fresh chopped oregano
1 pinch ground cinnamon
1 pinch ground cloves
1 teaspoon ground cumin
1 teaspoon salt
2-3 cloves fresh garlic (minced)
½ cup apple cider vinegar

Mix all ingredients with pork
Brown pork (chorizo) in a sauce pan or skillet on medium heat until done.

Serve!

Keeps well in the fridge but will stain your plasticware.

Chorizo Stuffed Squash Blossoms

This is another recipe I thought my kids would boycott, but they ended up liking it.

Squash blossoms are available seasonally. Figure out what season matters in your part of the world, and plan accordingly!

Ingredients:

Large bouquet of squash blossoms (we buy them from a nearby Mexican grocery store)
Chorizo (see recipe)
½ cup shredded cheese (Monterey jack or similar)
½ cup of gluten free flour
1/2 cup masa
¼ tsp garlic salt
¼ tsp cumin
4 eggs
1 cup gluten free panko
¼ cup corn oil
½ cup water

Brown the chorizo and mix with the cheese.

Warm the corn oil over medium-high heat.

Sift gluten free flour, masa, garlic salt and cumin together.

Whisk the eggs.

Put flour mix, eggs, water, and panko into separate bowls.

Stuff the chorizo cheese mixture into squash blossoms (wash and dry the squash blossoms first), then dip in (1) water, (2) flour mix (3) egg and (4) panko.

Fry in oil over medium-high heat, turning as needed 2-3 minutes per side until golden.

Serve immediately with salsa, guacamole, sour cream, and mint chutney.

Unfortunately, they don't keep so EAT UP!

Pickled Red Onions

1 red onion
½ cup apple cider vinegar
1 tablespoon sugar
1 ½ teaspoon salt
1 cup hot or warm water

Slice the red onion thinly and stuff into a glass jar with a lid. Cram it in there, as much as will fit. A canning jar works nicely.

Combine vinegar, salt, sugar and water. Stir to dissolve and pour carefully over the onions all the way to the top of the glass jar. Let them sit for 1 hour. After that hour, cover and store in the fridge.

Chilaquiles

Real chilaquiles are probably awesome but I don't know because I haven't tried them.

This is our favorite way to eat leftover Mexican restaurant food
the next morning for breakfast.

I usually order Tacos de Chorizo when I eat Mexican, because I like the taste and because it typically comes with corn tortillas rather than flour tortillas.

I eat one taco and save the other two, with all of the leftover tortilla chips, salsa, queso fresco, beans and rice.

I just dump it all into a to go container with the tortilla chips on top and stick it in the fridge.

Ingredients:
Fresh or stale tortilla chips
Jar of your favorite salsa (use at least 6 oz)
½ cup heavy cream or mexican crema
Fresh cilantro (chopped)
Pickled red onions (see recipe)
Chorizo (see recipe and/or use your favorite Mexican restaurant Tacos de Chorizo leftovers)
Queso fresco
Eggs

Pour salsa and cream over some of the tortilla chips in a big, deep skillet. Dump in your Mexican restaurant leftovers and/or chorizo. Heat over medium-high heat until the mixture is warm and bubbly. Crumble the rest of the tortilla chips over the mixture and sprinkle some queso fresco on top. Reduce heat to low.

Heat a second skillet and spray with cooking spray. Make over-easy eggs (two at a time) and serve over the chilaquiles with pickled red onions, queso fresco, and cilantro.

YUM!

Garlicky Salad Dressing

Zest of 1 lemon
Juice of 1 lemon
6-8 minced garlic cloves
Herbs de provence
White pepper
Equal parts honey, olive oil, and apple cider vinegar
Minced fresh parsley
Minced fresh mint

Don't refrigerate for best flavor

Use within a week

Goes good with kale and other rabbit food

If you need to visit salad jail on occasion, this is a tasty homemade gluten-free dressing.

Kale Salad

Yes, kale can taste good. It is good for you and should be eaten. It has such a strong flavor that it needs a strong dressing to counter-act the celery-like bitterness. This isn't salad jail; this is healthy rabbit food that actually tastes good.

Torn kale leaves (not the stems)
Mixed greens
Walnuts (whole or pieces)
Raspberries
Blueberries
Diced onion (white or yellow)

Dressing:

Olive oil
Honey
Herbs de provence
White pepper
Apple cider vinegar

You can eat them if you want, but I throw the kale stems out.

Go easy on the apple cider vinegar, but don't leave it out. I think it provides a nice counter balance to the bitterness of the kale. Just don't use more apple cider vinegar than honey. They should be equal proportions or heavy on the honey.

Can substitute diced apples for either the blueberries or the raspberries. Or add them in as a third fruit.

Don't sub out the walnuts.

Kids will even choke it down if you promise them a peanut butter chocolate chip cookie or a slice of turtle cheesecake.

GF Peanut Butter Chocolate Chip Cookies

It's a lot of sugar, but when gluten hates you, the treat foods are kinda lost. The gluten free treats that I have found in stores usually taste stale and bland. These cookies are very tasty.

1/2 tsp salt
2 large egg whites
1 cup creamy peanut butter
1 cup of whatever type of fancy chunky peanut butter you like (we used B. Happy PB Count Your Blessings brand for the picture but any brand will work if it's fancy, and chunky)
1/3 cup cane sugar
1/3 cup coconut palm sugar
1/2 cup brown sugar
Chocolate chips, M&Ms or similar coated chocolate candy, and/or broken pieces of a chocolate bar

Preheat oven to 375 degrees F.

Mix salt and egg whites with a wire whisk until frothy. Add in the two peanut butters, the sugars, and chocolate chips & M&Ms and mix it all up with a wooden spoon or spatula.

Divide up the dough into tablespoon size portions. Arrange on a baking sheet lined with parchment paper. I love parchment paper. It is a great tool to save time washing baking sheets. Also makes it super easy to get the cookies off the hot baking sheet efficiently so they can cool faster.

If you want to get fancy, you can use a fork to make criss cross marks on the dough balls. Just flatten them out a bit before you bake them because they really don't flatten out like regular cookies. They sort of stay in the shape you make them before baking. I like the criss cross – reminds me of school lunches in elementary school – except that these cookies kick ass!

Bake at 375 degrees F for 9 or 10 minutes or until they are lightly browned. Using the parchment paper, drag them off the cookie sheet onto a cookie rack to cool. After they've cooled, move them one by one to a plastic container with a lid, separating the layers with parchment paper so they don't stick together. Refrigerate.

Makes about 3 dozen cookies.

You won't believe me until you've tried it, but these cookies taste best after being refrigerated. And they keep nicely.

Turtle Cheesecake

2 cups of gluten free chocolate cookie crumbs (they look like Oreos, but are the gluten free version). You can leave in the white middles or scrape them out. I've done it both ways and it tastes good with the white part in and with the white part removed.
1 cup finely chopped pecans, divided
6 tablespoons butter, melted (NOT MARGARINE)
1 bag caramels, unwrapped
½ cup milk
3 8-ounce packages of cream cheese bricks, softened
¾ cup granulated or cane sugar
1 tablespoon vanilla
some semi sweet chocolates (bars or chips)
3 eggs

To make the crust:

Crunch up the gluten free cookies. I do this by sticking them all in a gallon freezer bag and beating on them with one of those meat hammers. Kids love this job.
Add in ½ cup pecans
Add in 6 tablespoons of melted butter

Mix all and squish onto the bottom and 2 inches up the sides of a 9-inch cheese cake pan.

Place caramels and milk in a microwaveable bowl. Microwave on high for 30 seconds, stir, then again on high 30 seconds, stir, etc. until the caramels are melted. Pour half of the melted caramel mixture onto the crust. Refrigerate the other half.

Refrigerate the crust for at least 10 minutes so the caramel hardens.

Let the cream cheese sit out at least 1 hour to soften. Preheat the oven to 300 degrees F.

Beat the cream cheese, sugar and vanilla in a mixer until blended. I use the medium setting so it doesn't splatter. Add in the eggs, one at a time, mixing on low after each egg is added so it is just blended.

Pour the batter over your caramel-gluten free cookie crust.

Bake at 300 degrees F for 60 minutes. Look, insert a toothpick, and cook a bit longer until almost set. Take it out if it develops a crack. OK if it cracks, but better if you get it out before that happens.

Let it cool for a few minutes, then run a butter knife around the sides to loosen it from the pan.

Let it cool completely, then remove the sides of the pan.

Refrigerate at least 4 hours, or overnight.

In the morning, microwave the rest of the caramel mixture and pour carefully over your cheesecake.

Sprinkle with pecans. Melt some of the chocolate and drizzle over the cheesecake. Sprinkle bits of chocolate, any leftover cookie crumbles, etc.

Cut carefully and serve. Store leftovers in the fridge or you can freeze it.

YUM.

Cream Cheese Icing

Kids love love love this and it's easy to make

1 brick of cream cheese – room temperature
1 stick of butter – room temperature (I know, I know, NOT MARGARINE)
3 cups of powdered sugar
1 teaspoon vanilla extract
1/8 teaspoon salt

Mix the cheese & butter using your stand mixer, then add in the sugar, vanilla, and salt.

Serve on cake, brownies, etc.

You can put it in the fridge, but it will turn solid. Still tastes good, but needs to sit out on the counter top or visit the microwave briefly if you want to spread it on something later.

Roasted Chicken

I bought a chicken at the grocery store the other day for $3.48. A whole chicken. A chicken's life is worth just $3.48. Odd to think of it that way. This chicken recipe is a great one to use for "starter" chicken for other recipes like white chicken chili and chicken & rice soup.

Whole fresh chicken, insides/giblets removed
Handful of fresh sage leaves
Handful of fresh lavender
Handful of fresh rosemary
Handful of fresh thyme
Quartered white or yellow onion (NOT RED ONION AND NOT VIDALIA ONION)
Quartered lemon
Salt & pepper

Rinse the chicken and throw away the stuff inside it (giblets or whatever that crap is).
Stuff the chicken with the fresh herbs, quartered onion, and two quarters of lemon.
Tuck 1 quarter of the lemon under each wing. I am not positive this makes it taste better but it sure looks funny.

Sprinkle liberally with salt and pepper.

Roast the chicken breast-side down in a clay pot for 5-6 hours or until your meat thermometer says it's done.

SAVE THE LIQUID

Pull the chicken apart and remove all of the bones. Remove the herbs and lemon rinds and discard.

You can pull the chicken out of the broth and separate them, but save that broth!

I chop up the onion that was roasted with the chicken and save it too.

Yummy by itself or in other dishes.

White Chicken Chili

Use some of your roasted chicken and the chicken broth in this dish.

Chicken
Chicken broth
2 cans of great northern beans + bean juice from the cans
1 chopped onion + the roasted chopped onion
1 small can of diced hatch chilis
Handful of cilantro leaves

Put all in a crock pot with a bit of water and cook all day on low.

Serve.

Keeps well in the fridge.

Good leftovers

Chicken & Rice Soup

Kids wouldn't stop eating this – it was gone the day I made it!

Use your roasted chicken and the chicken broth in this recipe

Chicken
Chicken broth
Roasted chopped onion
1 cup of grated carrots
1 cup of wild rice
Fresh thyme leaves
Fresh parsley leaves
1 bay leaf
Salt
½ cup heavy cream
Butter pats

Heat all in sauce pan over low-medium heat (except butter pats) for a while until wild rice is cooked (consult wild rice package for minimum time). Add melted butter pat to each serving. Eat!

I am pretty sure it would've kept well in the fridge but there wasn't any left for leftovers.

Stacey's Cooking Advice and some randomness on GLUTEN

Don't bother measuring every damn thing. Just eyeball it. That way you aren't spending all of your time rinsing/washing measuring cups and spoons. Close enough is good enough most of the time when it comes to measuring of ingredients.

Go light on salt unless my recipe says otherwise – in most situations you can always add more later. You can't easily fix dishes that were over-salted.

Add a sprinkle of nutmeg to nearly everything. OK everything. Like most all of everything you cook. Nutmeg – in moderation – ROCKS!

Experiment. When I want to make a new dish that I haven't made in the past, I consult a bunch of recipes to see the types of ingredients and preparation techniques that are commonly used, then I make up my own recipe. I never follow a recipe exactly. There is always something I am missing, something I don't like about the recipe, etc. I always experiment. If an experiment ends badly, just throw it away. Move on. Go to a Mexican restaurant and get Tacos de Chorizo with a margarita or two, then be the hero in the morning with chilaquiles!

A fool with a tool is still a fool. I don't really like kitchen gadgets. I've had bunches of them gifted to me over the years but don't really care for them. I like the mini chopper. And you can't go wrong with a good quality food processor. A nice set of knives, with a sharpener, is necessary, and I like having multiple cutting boards. Crappy ones that I don't mind staining, and good ones for SHOW. Fo SHOW! Definitely you need a really nice cast iron skillet. Nothing like it! I like having the stand mixer, but hate how big it is, how much counter space it takes up. And that clay pot. We got that from some zany fun work lady at our wedding, and were perplexed at what it was and why it was gifted (nothing like it was on our wedding registry). Best gift ever! We use it often, and love every dish that comes from its use.

Most of the rest of it is just clutter. The potato ricer. The mandolin. The rice cooker. A dozen other devices that claim to make your prep/cooking experience faster. Whatever time you save using the device to prepare your dish, you will waste cleaning it and all of its pieces later.

I always do the cleaning while I am doing the cooking so that when it's time to eat, I can just sit down, relax and enjoy eating without having to worry about cleaning up afterwards.

Oh, and advice about spices and seasonings. Taste stuff singly and in combination. Combos can be great, but too many different flavors in combination can break, not make, a recipe. Think how each spice tastes before you add it in. Experiment first. Keep the five tastes in mind: salty, sweet, bitter, sour, and savory (Umami). Savory is my favory. Read about savory, and do some savory taste testing, because you may find that it's the thing that sets your dishes apart. Isolate savory and use it the right way!

It took me years to eliminate enough gluten from my diet that my insides started working right again. These gluten free recipes are ones I am proud to share with my family and friends. Nobody suspects that they are eating a "gluten sensitive" dish, and I don't broadcast it because people seem to think if the gluten is missing that it might not taste as good. Not true!

I do still miss a good yeast roll. Nothing quite like it in the gluten free market that I can find. Cake wasn't ever my favorite, and fresh-made gluten free cookies aren't ever as tasty right out of the oven as the regular kind. I don't enjoy a good cheeseburger anymore because gluten-free buns really suck. Still. Seems like somebody could've gotten that right by now.

Eating out is always a crap shoot. Literally. Even if you order a gluten free dish, the chain of custody has to remain intact for you to actually RECEIVE the gluten free version of whatever it is that you ordered. Not everybody is careful. It has to get from the server to the kitchen staff to the person who stages the completed food for pickup to the person who delivers it to your table (which may not be your original server). Many times I've ordered a dish at a restaurant and very carefully, politely emphasized that it needs to be gluten free, only to receive it with a regular bun rather than a gluten free bun if it's a sandwich, a roll on the side if it is a steak dish, croutons strewn on top if it's a salad, served with flour tortillas rather than corn tortillas, etc etc etc. You have to be your own advocate and make sure it's clear that everyone making the food and delivering the food knows the importance of getting you the gluten free version.

Some restaurants like to make the gluten free version look just like the regular version. This is a mistake, because of that chain of custody thing I mentioned. Everybody needs to be able to identify the gluten free version, from the server to the kitchen staff to the folks delivering it to your table, to you. I can't always tell by looking at a dish that it's gluten free. At this point, I can mostly tell if it's gluten free when I taste it, but not always. I always know later. At times, it takes multiple days to recover if I am served something with gluten in it. Small amounts aren't so bad, like if I happen to eat food that is fried in a fryer alongside breaded foods. A whole piece of bread, however, sets me back a good 3-4 days. Once, I ordered what I thought was a gluten free grilled cheese sandwich (TWO pieces of bread). When it was delivered to me, I took a bite, and asked the server to confirm that I actually received the gluten free version. It just tasted too good. She, of course, said "yes, it is gluten free," but at my insistence, went back to the kitchen to confirm. The cook came out and confirmed to me that it was gluten free, and told me she knew how good it was. That it tasted like the real thing. I believed both of them, and ate the grilled cheese. I missed two days of work and didn't recover from the grilled cheese (which was NOT gluten free) for a total of 11 days. It was the worst kind of awful. I will never, ever, ever, trust a grilled cheese from a restaurant again. Totally not worth it.

Soy sauce is another tricky monster. It is NOT gluten free. The second ingredient in regular soy sauce is wheat. Took me forever to figure out why I felt like shit after eating sushi. I assumed it was the rice, but found out too late that it was the soy sauce. I now bring my own packets of GF soy sauce to sushi restaurants; and I usually eat sashimi to ensure no soy sauce is added.

Getting out of salad jail - and staying out of salad jail - takes a lot of work.

It's worth it!

Not only do I like cooking, but I also enjoy getting to eat the same dinner as the rest of my family vs. eating a bland restaurant salad while they all enjoy a creamy pasta dish, a creative appetizer, or a decadent dessert.

Happy eating!

Made in the
USA
Monee, IL